CW00505291

The Sensual
Midlife

Rylan James

BookLeaf
Publishing

The Sensual Side of Midlife © 2023 Rylan
James

All rights reserved.

No part of this publication may be
reproduced, stored in a retrieval system, or
transmitted, in any form or by any means,
electronic, mechanical, photocopying,
recording or otherwise, without the prior
written permission of the presenters.

Rylan James asserts the moral right to be
identified as author of this work.

Presentation by *BookLeaf Publishing*

Web: www.bookleafpub.com

E-mail: info@bookleafpub.com

ISBN: 9789357742627

First edition 2023

PREFACE

I cordially invite you to join me as I become the me that I want to be. I am powerful. I am passionate. I am brave. I bare my soul here, and I invite you to see it, feel it, imagine it.

And maybe, if you're brave, begin your own journey

The Edge

I've been on the edge for awhile now.

I've been looking for that feeling, any feeling really.

I've been numb.

I've been holding it all together and wondering if there's more to this life.

And now I've taken a leap, a giant leap off the edge and I'm falling.

I've fallen hard and irrevocably.

I've fallen so dramatically and beautifully that I no longer wonder if there's more to this life…I know that there is.

Shedding Fear

I've always worn my fear like a coat of armor.
I thought it kept me safe.
I thought it protected me. It felt bulky, yet
strong. It felt cold, yet cozy.
I've always worn my fear like a coat of armor.
I thought it kept me safe.

It did, to a degree. It kept me from getting my
heart broken. It also kept me from loving fully
and wildly.

It kept me from being rejected. It also kept me
from being accepted.
It kept me from failure. It also kept me from
success.
So I'm slowly shedding my armor…and I'm
scared and I'm excited. I'm nervous and
hopeful. I feel brave and empowered.
I've always worn my fear like a coat of armor.
I thought it kept me safe.

Now I know that it only kept me from living my
life fully and passionately, wildly and freely.

I'm shedding my armor. And it feels good.

That Long Lost Feeling

Scrolling for inspiration one day, I came upon some beautiful pieces of art that sparked a memory, well, less of a memory and more the remnants of a feeling long ago forgotten.

These images were nude women: curvy, colorful, serene and sensual. I kept looking at them, realizing more and more that I wanted to see myself reflected in those moods and models.

See, for years, I have been a caregiver, a maid, a secretary, a chef, and a chauffeur. I was anything but a woman, let alone a woman who wants to celebrate her curves and sexuality and simple beauty. I would like to think that I'm more than all those roles.

I am a woman who wants to feel bold in her skin, tender, and even sexy. I want to be at peace with myself and have it show in the way I carry myself.

I want that long lost feeling back.

Photograph

It's incredible what one photograph can tell you about yourself. Not just any photo, but the right photo, at the right time.

You see yourself in a new light, a gentle light, a light you've never seen before.

You see a wisp of hair, a freckle, a grin that tilts to one side…

You see an expression on your face, one that you had forgotten existed and before you know it, you long to be that woman again.

And just like that, everything has changed.
And just like that, the right photograph at the right time in just the right light has given you hope, a direction, a flicker of who you used to be and want to be again.

Unraveling

I've got this sweater, a sweater that I live in.
And when this sweater was first woven, it was
just right, just what I wanted it to be.

And all these years later, it's still warm and
comfortable, though it might be time to make
some adjustments…

I pull a couple stray threads and they unravel,
it's a bit challenging, seems to be coming along
though.

And then it's time to reweave that part. I'm
thoughtful about the color and texture, the
weave isn't too loose or too tight, it's just as I
want it to be.

As I pull another thread, I become excited about
the possibilities as I see what new yarns are
available, new patterns. I want my sweater to fit
the me that I am now.

I take my time, and it takes work. My hands
ache and my eyes are tired, but I've done it.

I unraveled all the parts of the sweater that no longer served me, and I have thoughtfully and painstakingly rewoven it to fit me better.

It's just right. It's just what I want it to be.

On the Water

Paddling on my favorite lake, today I made myself quake.
Rather bold of me, but something took ahold of me.

The sunlight, the sparkling water, the gentle waves…

The gentle rocking of my anchored boat, as I lean back and float.
I feel tingling everywhere, my skin exposed and bare.

The sunlight, the sparkling water, the gentle waves…

I tease my nipples, down my body sending ripples.
I slide my hand down, down, down, nestling in my mound.

The sunlight, the sparkling water, the gentle waves…

My fingers slide into the fold, feeling warm and wet and so bold.
I lean back and widen my legs, writhing as my body begs.

The sunlight, the sparkling water, the gentle waves...

My senses are ripe and my body is on fire, feeling like the quiet is no longer my desire.
I buck and moan, touching myself all alone.

The sunlight, the sparkling water, the gentle waves...

And I feel a warm rush as my body releases a gush.
My moans have become a sound shrill, then a breath held still.

And I lean back and enjoy the current that flows through my body, and I bask in the sunlight, the sparking water, the gentle waves....

Do you feel it?

You knock on my door, I let you in and we shake
hands.

Do you feel it?

We conduct our business sitting across from
each other at the dining room table.

Do you feel it?

I walk you to the door, you smile and so do I.

Do you feel it?

We shake hands again.

And then I know you feel it

Arapaima

You open the door and come inside. You take off your boots and sit down next to me. You lean my way, put your feet up. I channel surf and we land on the story of the Amazonian fish, the arapaima.

You don't seem comfy so I urge you to get cozy. You scoot my way and put your head on my breast. I lift my arm and rest it on your chest while my other hand rakes the top of your head. You tell me that you like that.

Before I know it, you are touching the top of my hand with yours, stroking your thumb back and forth. Your body has turned ever so slowly my way, your face as well.

My breath hitches as I lay my head on your chest and slide your way a bit...my lips close to your chin, as my head leans in the opposite direction.

And slowly, your lips are closer to mine, and I feel whiskers, then smooth lips as we kiss quickly, briefly...and then I feel warmth and a sense of giddiness that I had forgotten...and I'm smiling.

And now whenever I hear the word arapaima, I think of that night, of the intimate moments, and the heat.

On the Cusp…

We hold hands and walk around the corner of the building. We dodge the cameras and I press myself into a corner, and I pull you close.

I unzip your jacket despite the cold, and slide my hands in while your hands circle my waist. My breathing is rapid as I try to say what's on my mind, what I've been feeling for awhile now…

I look into your beautiful brown eyes and I tell you, "I think I'm falling in love with you."

You smile your handsome smile, and you pull me closer and kiss me, gentle and slow. Before I know it, I'm greedily tasting your lips and and pulling on your coat collar. You come closer to me so willingly that I knock my head on the wall and all I can think is that I want to bite your lip, your ear, your neck.

I wrap one leg around you trying to get as close to you as I can, wishing there was nothing between our bodies but sweat and heat.

And this is just the beginning…

One

I take your hand and pull you to the couch. We
face each other and I push you to sit down. I
straddle you and wrap my arms around your
neck.

And we breathe. Just breathe and feel the way
our bodies are connected and in sync with each
other. Your arms are wrapped around me, your
hands resting on my lower back. My hands
caress the back of your neck and your shoulders
gently.

Eventually I feel our cheeks pressed lightly
together. I'm unaware that either of us has
moved, and yet…before I realize what's
happening, our mouths are timidly migrating
toward each other. We stop ourselves briefly
when we are millimeters away from the
kiss…and then we give in. And we are one.
One body, one heart, one burning soul…

A Morning at the Beach

It's early in the day, and I'm sitting in my chair on my favorite beach. I'm wearing long sleeves and leggings, and my favorite wide brimmed sun hat.

I'm listening to the waves roll in as I try to read a book, but the sky and waves captivate me and keep me from my book.

And then I see what I think is a young man wander to the edge of the water. He sheds his shoes and his shirt, stacking them neatly on the sand.

He begins moving his body on the beach, a mix of boxing and dance. His skin and muscles gleam in the sunlight despite his dark mahogany color.

I'm mesmerized as I watch the swells in his arms, his abdomen, his back. He works his way into the water, ankle deep, the small splashes as he moves are rhythmic and somehow musical.

And when he's had enough of the water, he walks up the sand, gathering his things, and glances my way…and I smile as I see just how beautiful his body is up close…and I'm in a trance as he says hello with his plump lips and sexy accent, sparkly eyes and deep voice.

The Bath

You and I lay together in bed, our bodies slick with
sweat.
Your hand is on my leg, and my hand covers yours.
You turn and give me a peck on top of my head, and
walk into the bathroom.
I hear the water come on, loud and rushing, the
bathtub perhaps?
You sprinkle epsom salts as you fill the tub, and I can
smell the lavender scent mixed in.
You get in and I'm not sure if I should join you, but
then you beckon me.
Facing each other, our legs wrap together like a
cinnamon twist and we each lean back and soak in
the fizzy bath water.
You reach for me and we link hands across the tub,
alongside our interwoven knees, and just breathe in
the lavender.
My breasts are barely covered by the water and
they've got a bit of a chill, nipples erect.
I feel so warm though, the water is like a massage on
my back, my hips, my bottom, my legs.
And I look at you, our fingers threaded together, and
you're smiling.

And I mirror you reflexively, leaning my head back,
eyes closed, smiling.

I See You

You rush over and slump down on the floor against a granite tiled column. You are talking on the phone to your mom while scarfing down a salad.

You're a bit of a mess, but the way you talk to your mom captures my attention as I try to pretend I'm not eavesdropping.

Later I'm on the plane and think I have an empty seat next to me when you breeze on in and sit next to me. As I begin to get anxious for the flight, you listen to music and just seem so chill.

And then I can't breathe. I feel closed in and like I'm falling at the same time. I reach for whatever is next to me and you are startled when I grasp your arm. And that one second of contact brings me back. I brace myself and force my breath to resume its normal rhythm.

And then I feel like a fool, and you are so kind with your friendly smile and your warm green eyes. Turns out you are a helper, a natural generous soul who knows how to distract me from my embarrassment, reviving my dignity with your grace. You know how to calm me.

And you do. Until you don't. My heart is racing for much more enjoyable reasons as we hold hands and breathe together, as I awaken in you what has already been stirring in me.

And I see you, all of you. Your kind heart and your beautiful eyes, even your 70's pornstar mustache...I see you.

Where will I find you?

I'm here, I'm here, standing in the large room in
the old English house…with the dim lighting
and the crackling fire, the thick rug
beckoning…the large windows giving us a sense
of being on display despite the darkness.

And tomorrow, where will I find you?

I've walked into your office and you aren't here.
I look out to the hall and it's empty, no sign of
you…
I wander in taking in the scent of you, the
masculine feel of the decor, the tidy workspace
that echoes fingers typing, notes made, calls
answered.
I sit in your chair, feeling like I'm gaining a
glimpse into your world...I lean back in the chair
and close my eyes and think of you and "our
work" yet to be conducted…

And where will I find you the next day?

You will find me in a posh hotel, in a room with
a four poster bed, lavish linens and a luxurious
bathroom with a large glass shower just big
enough…you will spoil me all day and all

night…we will giggle and play and tell stories and share our favorite things and we will dream about all that might come in the future

Where will I find you, you ask?

In your heart, in your soul, in your eyes and in your arms.

Coming Home

I remember when we'd all sit smooshed on the couch watching tv.

I remember when we'd all play video games in the den taking turns sitting on the cushions.

I remember having snowball fights in winter, and swimming in the summer.

I remember climbing trees and exploring the barn.

I remember board games and dinners and neighbors.

I remember connection and shared experiences and watching you grow up.

I remember feeling like you were slipping away and then you were gone.

I remember trying to stay connected for awhile.

And then I remember distance, children, work, and struggle.

And now when I need you, you're here for me.

And it's like you've come home.

Arrival

I'm having an emotional day, and I'm driving
while talking to you on the phone. I am almost
to my destination so I pull into the lot of a closed
office building.

You hear the stress in my voice and you want to
distract me. You tell me to reach into my pants.
You tell me to touch myself. You tell me to keep
going and I do.

You listen to me, my breathy moans fill your
ears and you are aroused. And then I'm louder
and louder as the rush comes, and then again and
again…your voice is an aphrodisiac and I'm
overdosing on it.

And when it's over, we giggle and banter and
relish the spontaneity, and revel in our
relationship that allows for a little bit of
everything…

I've Got You

When I see you for the first time, I am shocked.
I am sad and shocked.

We are the same age, yet you look like you have
30 years on me.

Your face is lined with grief, your skin sunken
and pale.
Your frame shakes, and I feel your arms wrap
around me for a hug.
A warm and kind hug, a skin and bones hug, a
long and deep hug.
Your eyes tell me a story, one so solemn and
unnerving.

When you deserved companionship, you
suffered loneliness.
When you tried to be of help, you were used and
treated like a servant.
When you had love to give, it was treated as
weakness and shunned.

You're safe now, I've got you.

All the love and kindness and patience and
thoughtfulness and friendship and support you
deserve….
I've got you.

Flowers

I hold your face in my hands. Your hat has come off and I can see your hazel blue green eyes.

We breathe together, in sync without even trying. Your eyes are full of tears, the surface tension about to break and send a stream down your face.

You tell me that you've given up, you don't want to go on, life has been just too hard…

And in that moment, that second, I feel my heart about to burst and I tell you that it's time to love yourself.

The tears spill down your face and I'm telling you again that it's time to love yourself, and that you matter.

And the tears begin to slow, your eyes are open and looking into mine, and I feel it…you hear me and believe me when I tell you that you are worthy of love and kindness.

And then I know my heart grows, I can feel flowers blooming from it, sprouting in my chest and they want to come flying out of me to share with the world.

And I feel some flowers wanting to float through the house and spread to others…

And in that moment, I know you will live, thrive, and even bloom someday.

Shopping

Out shopping one day,
blue jeans calling me, asking for a say.

Blue jeans calling and calling,
 with rips and frays and quilling.
The most plain and boring of them all,
are finally found near the changing hall.

I hold your hand and pull you along,
 hoping and hoping the jeans fit like a song.
And these blue jeans go on smoothly,
and then again and again, I feel they fit truly.

As I prepare to put my own pants back on,
you pull me close, you kiss me and hold me so
long.
You hands can be felt on my hips,
while my hands find your lips.
I pull on one lip, toying a bit,
then I nipping a bit, kissing you, you touch my
tit.

I straddle your body as you sit on the bench,
you hold my ass tightly giving it a pinch.
And then we hear others,

and we giggle as we think of our mothers,

What would they say of us acting this way?

Closer

Your hands are in my hair, our foreheads are
touching, and I'm mesmerized by your lips.
We look into each others eyes and slowly our
mouths reach each other.
As our lips envelope each other, our eyes remain
connected, our bodies mimicking the motion of
our lips.
Our legs and arms are twisted up together,
wrapped and moving like lungs searching for
breath.
Your lips make their way to my neck while I
arch my back and lift my head giving you skin
to explore.
Your hands feverishly make their way around to
my ass and you plunge your hand down the back
of my pants, squeezing, caressing, dragging your
fingers down and then up the crevasse between
my cheeks.
My breath hitches and I realize I am aroused, for
the first time in what seems like forever.

And damn does it feel good.

Hungry

In a matter of days, I've become hungry for you. So
hungry to know everything about you.
Just when I think I've learned enough, more
questions surface. I can't get enough.
I want to know more and more. I'm hungry for it.

I want to know what makes you smile, I want to
know what makes you sad…
I want to feel what's in your heart and know what's
on your mind, and I want to drink it in.
And I'm hungry to touch your skin, to hear how you
got each scar, I want to memorize your body and
devour it at the same time.

I want to know more and more. I'm hungry for it.
I want to know what you love about yourself, how
you'd like to grow and what I can do to support you.
I want to know your hopes and dreams, and I want to
know what might be in store for us.

I want to know more and more. I'm hungry for it.
I want a long warm hug, and I want to hold your
hand.
I want to kiss your soft lips, your cheeks, your eyes.
I want to feel you pressed up against me, and then I
want to feel you inside me, I want to feel the heat and
the wetness and the shudders…

I want to hear both of us try to catch our breath, and revel in our perfect chemistry, and the way our bodies fit together so beautifully.

And more than anything, I want you to quench my thirst and satisfy that hunger, not just once, but forever and always.

Milton Keynes UK
Ingram Content Group UK Ltd.
UKHW020817150923
428743UK00015B/676